Step Oot Boldly

The Hidden Meaning of The Statue of Liberty

Written & Illustrated by
Darrell Fusaro

foozaro.com

STEP OUT BOLDLY: The Hidden Meaning of The Statue of Liberty
Copyright ©2024 by Darrell Fusaro. All rights reserved.
Printed in the United States of America.

This book or any portion thereof may not be reproduced or used in any manner whatsoever without the express written permission of the publisher except for the use of brief quotations in a book review. For information, ArtsRelease@me.com.

www.ThisWillMakeYouHappy.com

First Printing, 2024

ISBN 979 8 3396 7860 1

To my great-grandparents,
Pasquale and Cristina Fusaro.
They believed in a dream
and stepped out boldly.

When I need inspiration, I don't want to have to wade through a lot of text to get it. I want something brief to read that will ignite my enthusiasm and motivate me.

My intention in creating this short book is that you will be motivated by what Lady Liberty symbolizes enough to pursue your dream.

Symbolism is the art of sharing spiritual truths hidden in plain sight.

Understanding what symbols represent can provide us with clues to successful living.

The Statue of Liberty is loaded with symbolism that you can use to accomplish your goals and realize your desires.

The statue's actual name is "Liberty Enlightening the World."

Liberty, by definition, is a person's freedom from control by fate or necessity. Enlightening, or to enlighten, is to give someone spiritual knowledge or insight.

The title implies that the symbolism contained in this monument imparts a spiritual method by which we all can obtain our heart's desire regardless of our circumstances. So let's uncover the hidden meaning of the Statue of Liberty and discover what she embodies.

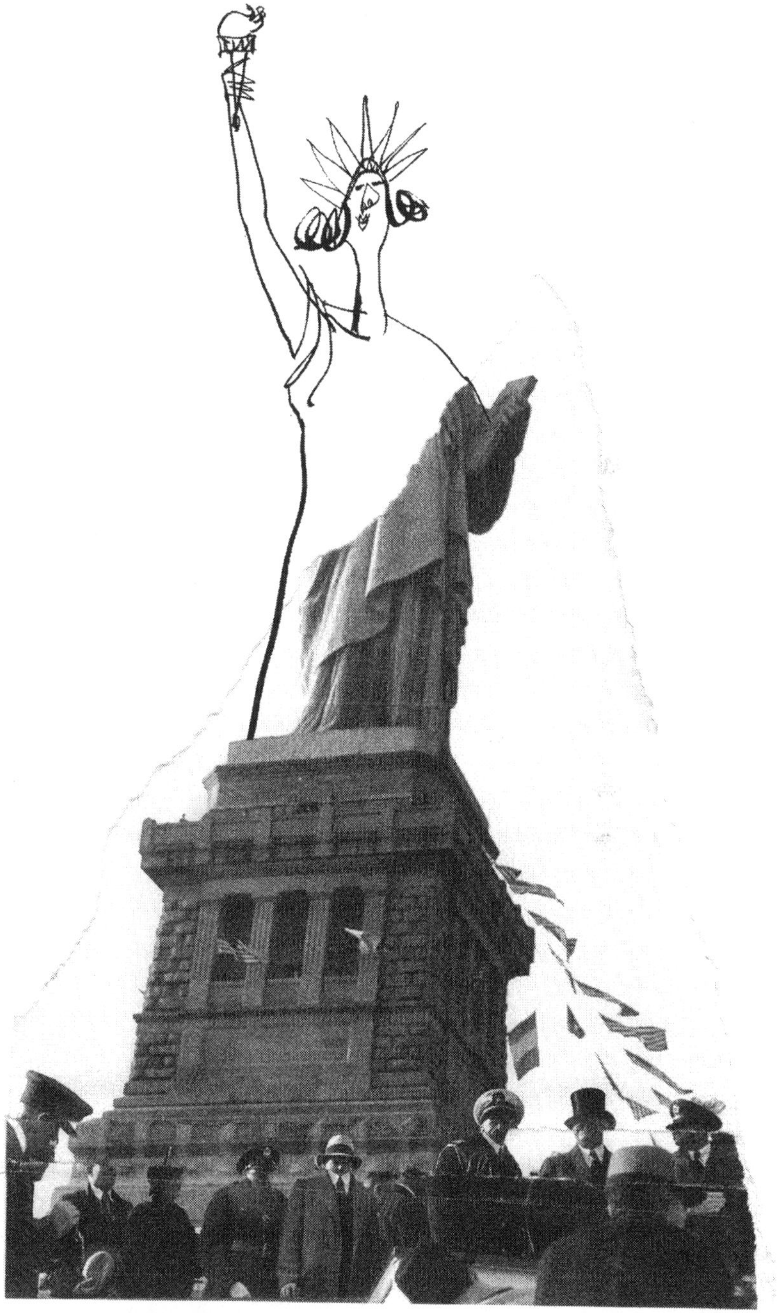

Did you know that the Statue of Liberty isn't standing still?

If you notice her right foot, you will see by its position that she's about to take a step forward.

The right side is symbolic of Truth and Power. Truth is our inner Divinity that is constantly inspiring, guiding, and motivating us to greater good. Power is our inherent ability to follow through on this Truth and take action.

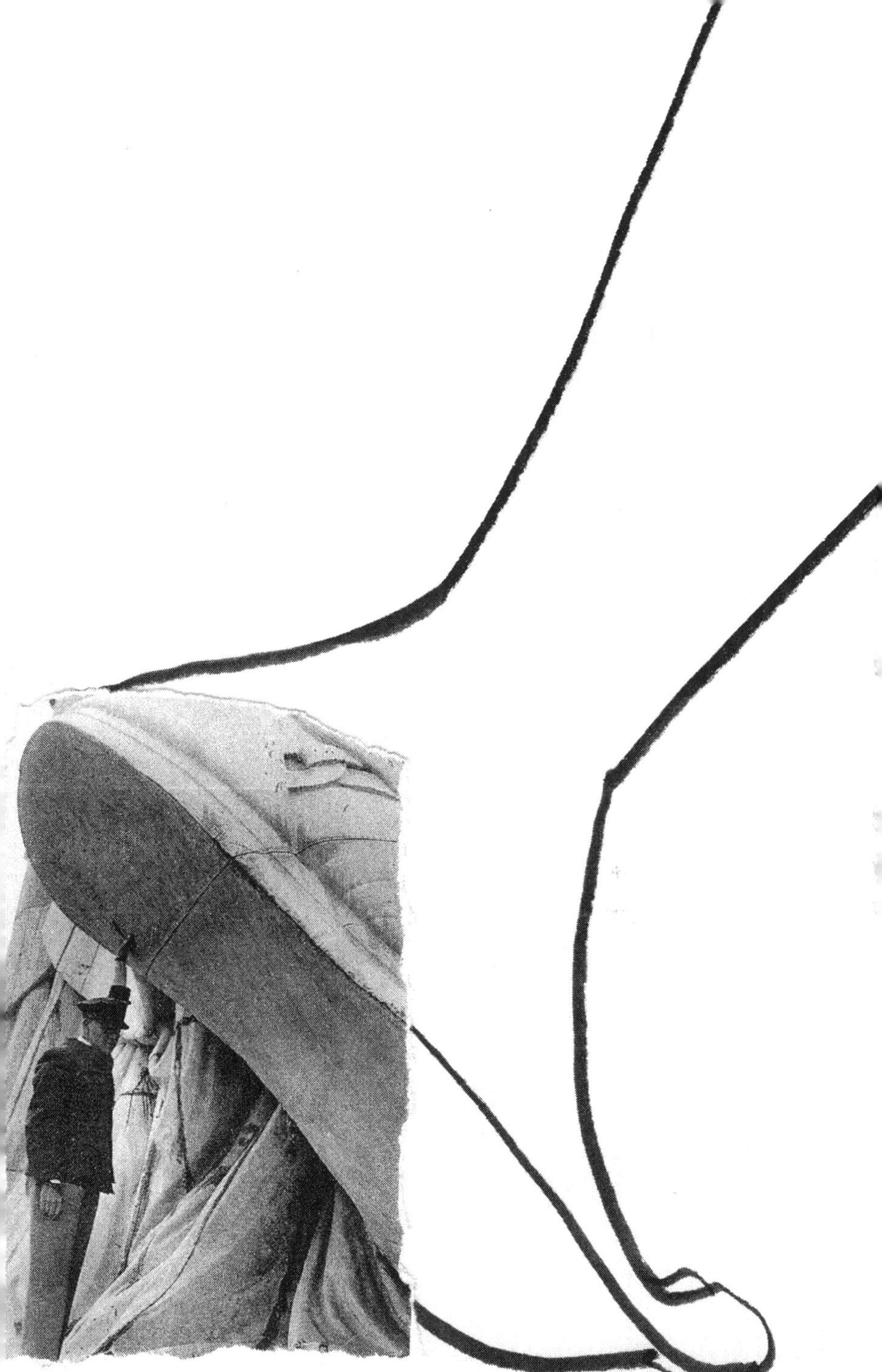

When viewing the statue's right side, it's clear by the draping of her gown that her right leg is in mid-stride.

With this, Lady Liberty demonstrates the fact that our true security lies in adventure.

When you step out of your comfort zone your confidence will rise to the occasion.

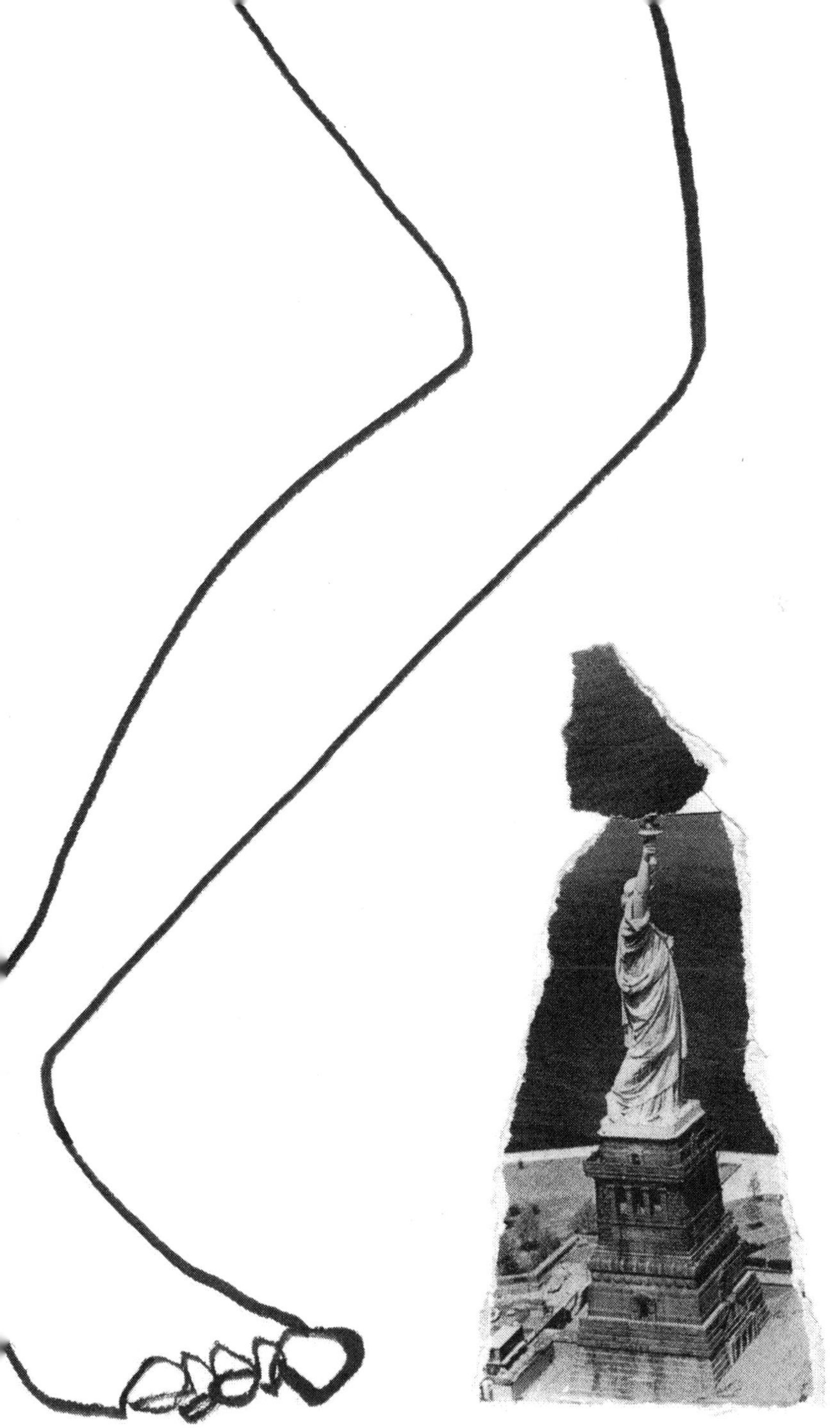

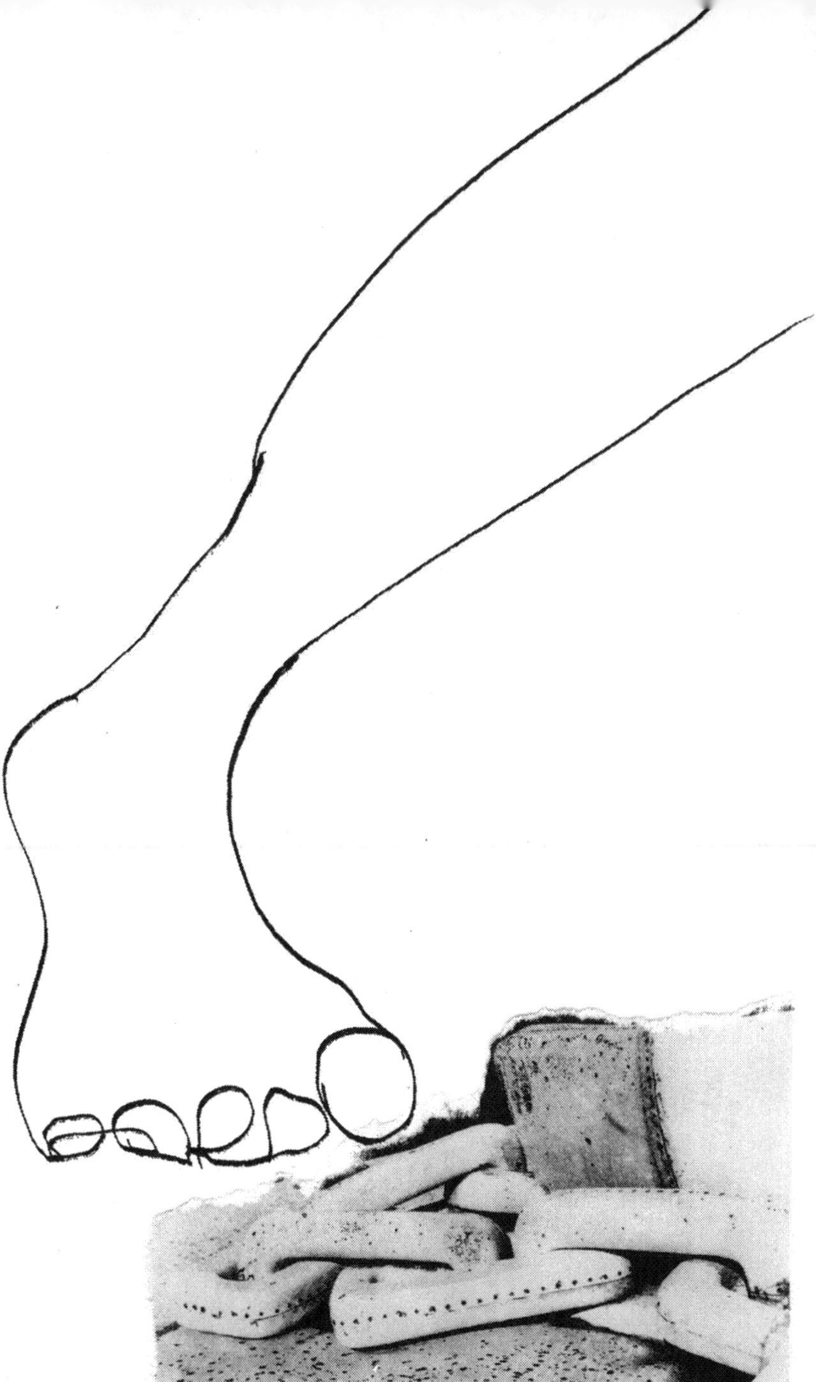

At her feet there are broken chains, representing freedom from oppression —the shackles of fear, doubt, and worry that often hinder us from taking that crucial first step toward our desires.

The mere act of taking that first step releases us from these shackles.

Whatever you desire to accomplish or achieve, just take the first step.

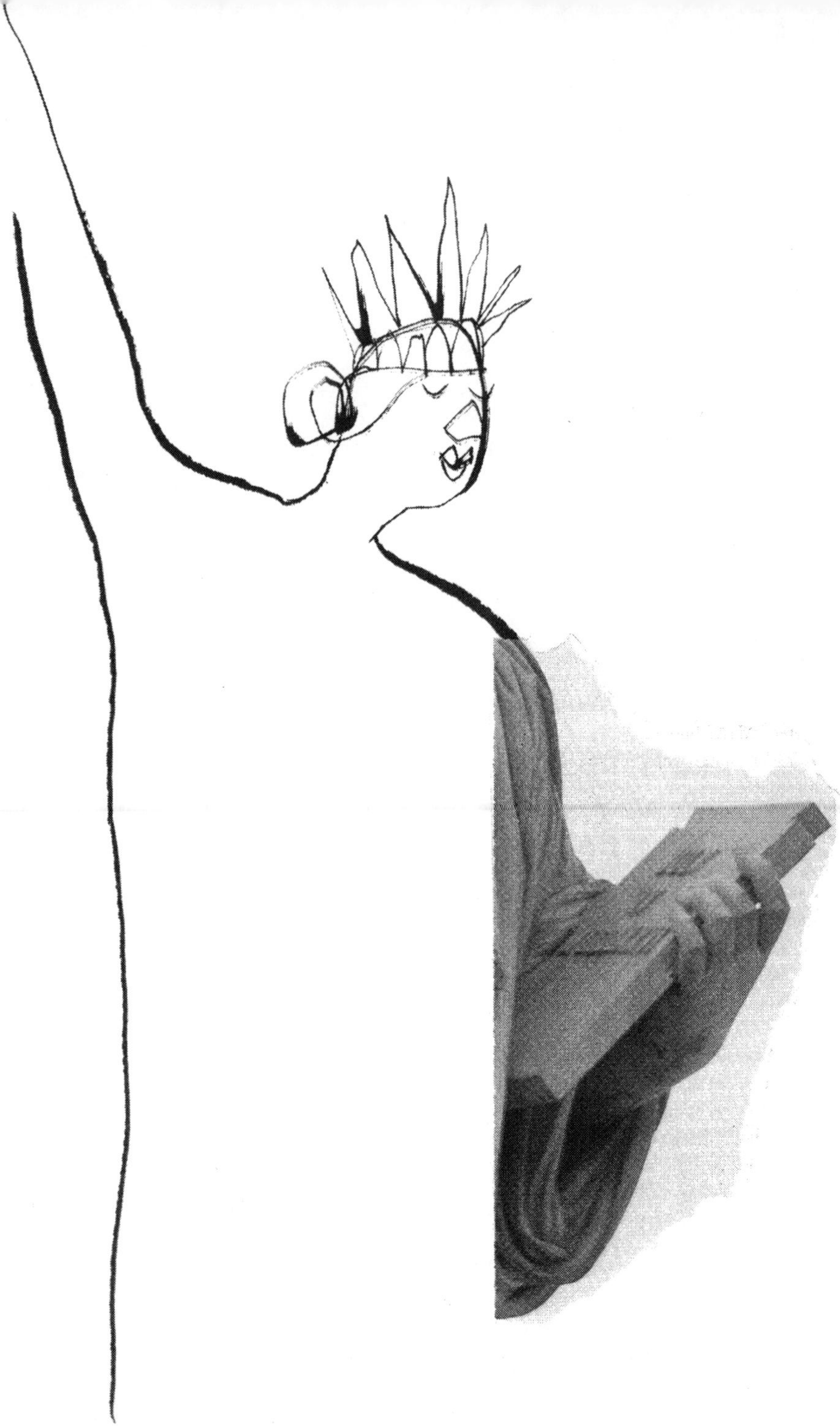

She holds a tablet inscribed with Roman numerals reading "July 4, 1776," symbolizing America's Declaration of Independence.

This highlights the truth that when you make a decision—your personal Declaration of Independence—to boldly take a step toward your desire, the Universe will conspire in your favor.

Results always follow decisions.
Things begin to happen that fall in line with our decisions.

Do this and Providence will illuminate your path, symbolized by the torch she holds high in her right hand.

This is the promise that as you move forward, you will be guided by your intuition—God in you—and it will never lead you astray.

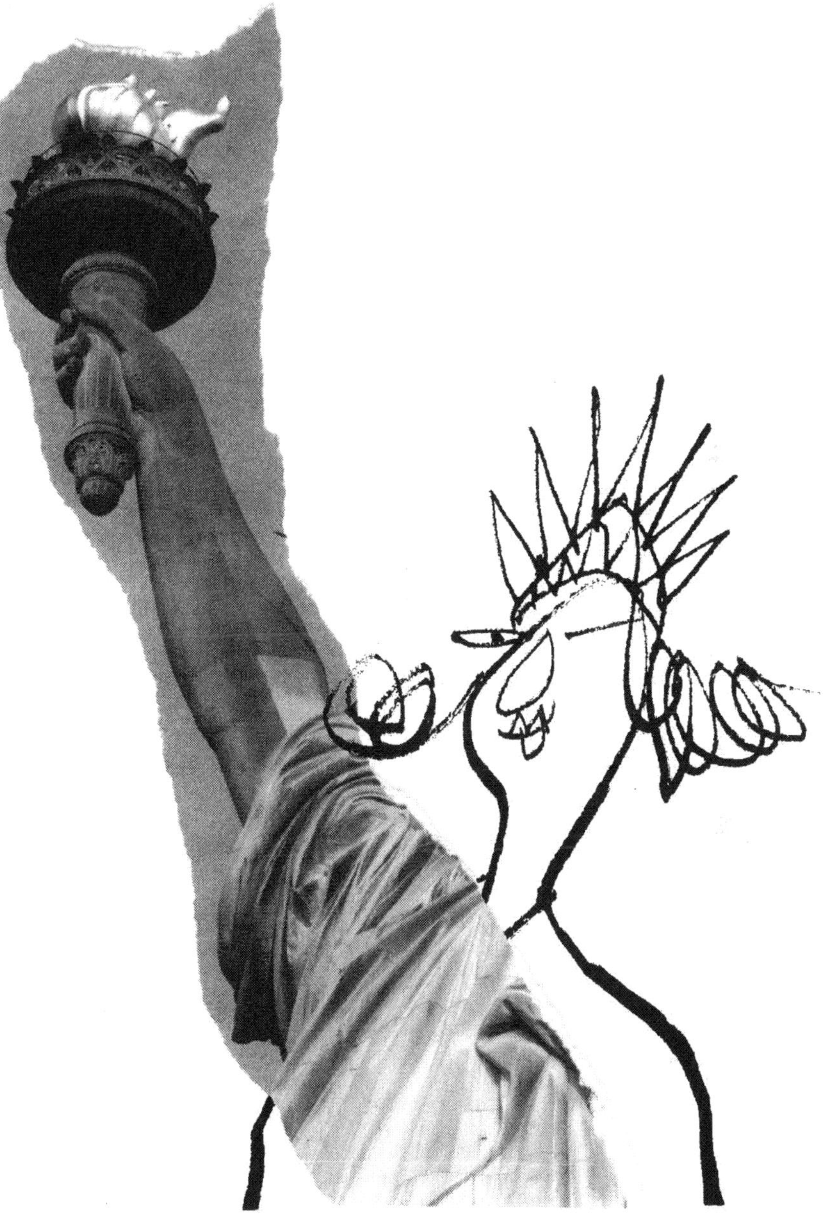

Liberty is represented as a woman. The woman or female is symbolic of our feeling nature.

She is a reminder that our liberty and success are not obtained by force but rather by way of our thoughts and feelings.

This is the encouragement to go forth with faith and love—to step forward with joyful expectation.

When our imagination is fueled with a loving enthusiasm for our desire, we are propelled toward it and we attract opportunity.

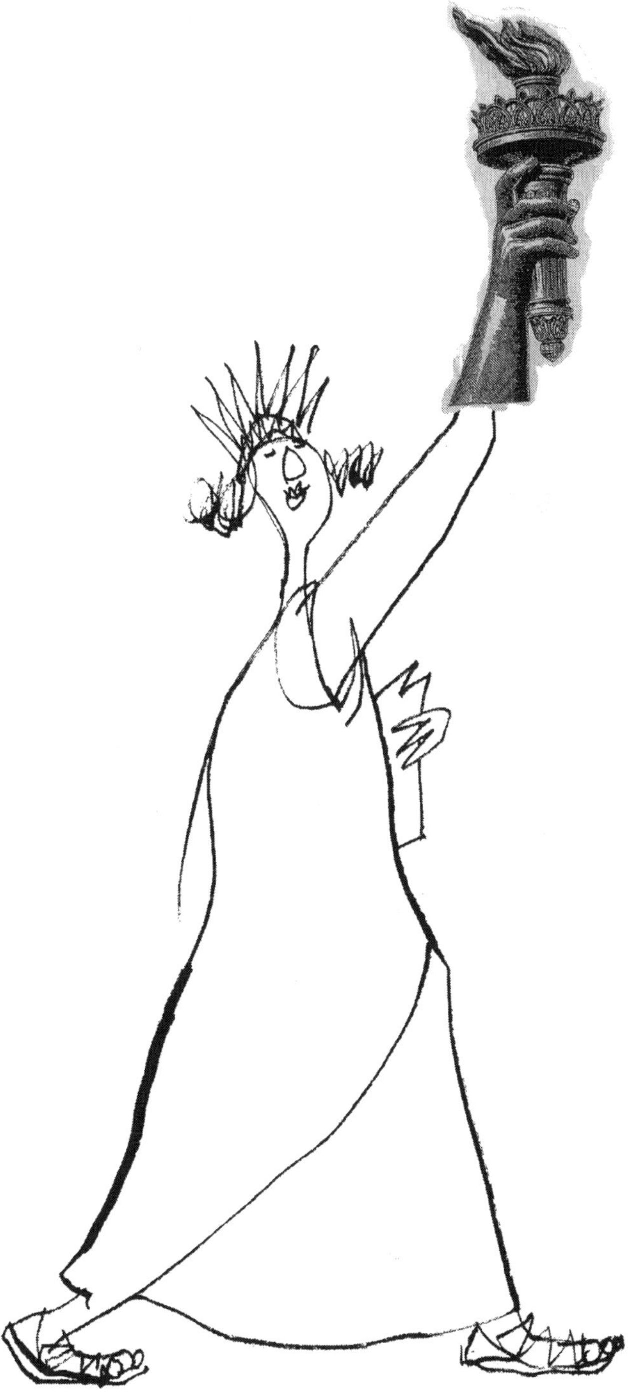

1.
2.
3.
4.
5.
6.
7.

When we take a step in the direction of our desire, we are crowned with favor just as she is.

By choosing to follow the promptings of our heart we feel empowered, enthusiastic, and radiant.

The seven points, which are rays of light atop her crown symbolize this state of consciousness.

When we let our light shine, we inspire others to do the same.

The fact that there are seven rays underscores the universality of Liberty's enlightening message as being applicable to everyone across all seven continents and the seven seas.

Lady Liberty emphasizes the spiritual truth that you can embark on the transformative journey toward realizing your dreams regardless of who you are or where you are when you step out boldly.

Every immigrant who stepped aboard a ship destined for the United States of America during the nineteenth and twentieth centuries embodied these principles to the point of action.

Most came with nothing but their belief in what Liberty promised.

With that many succeeded.

So can you.

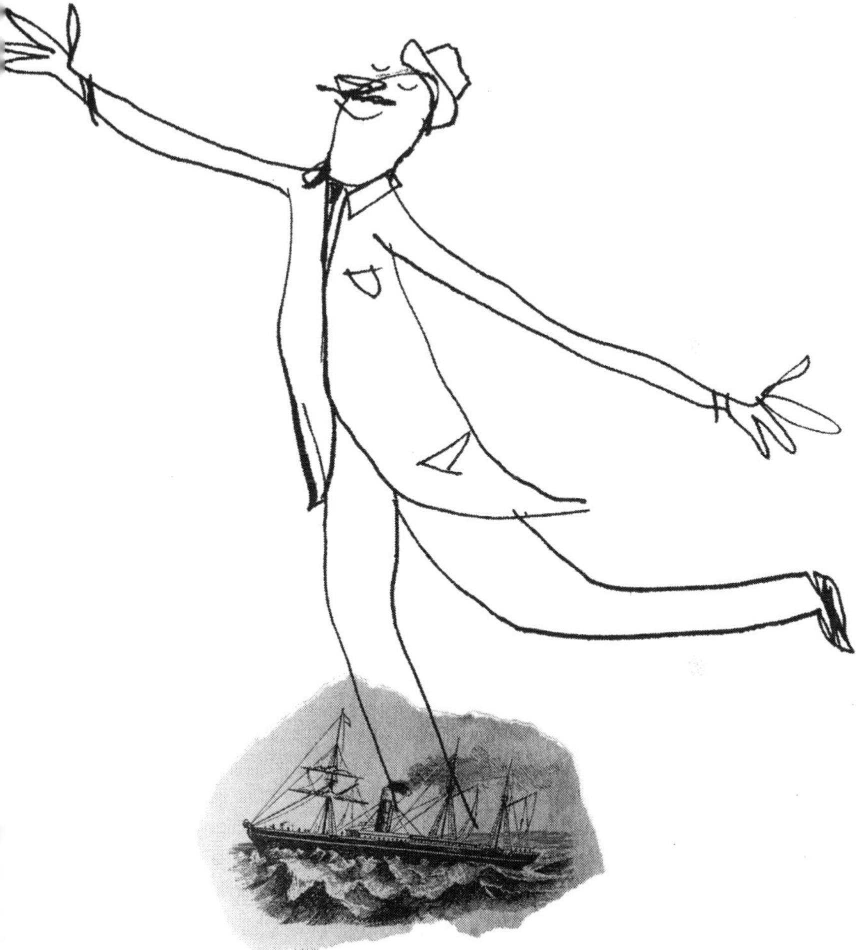

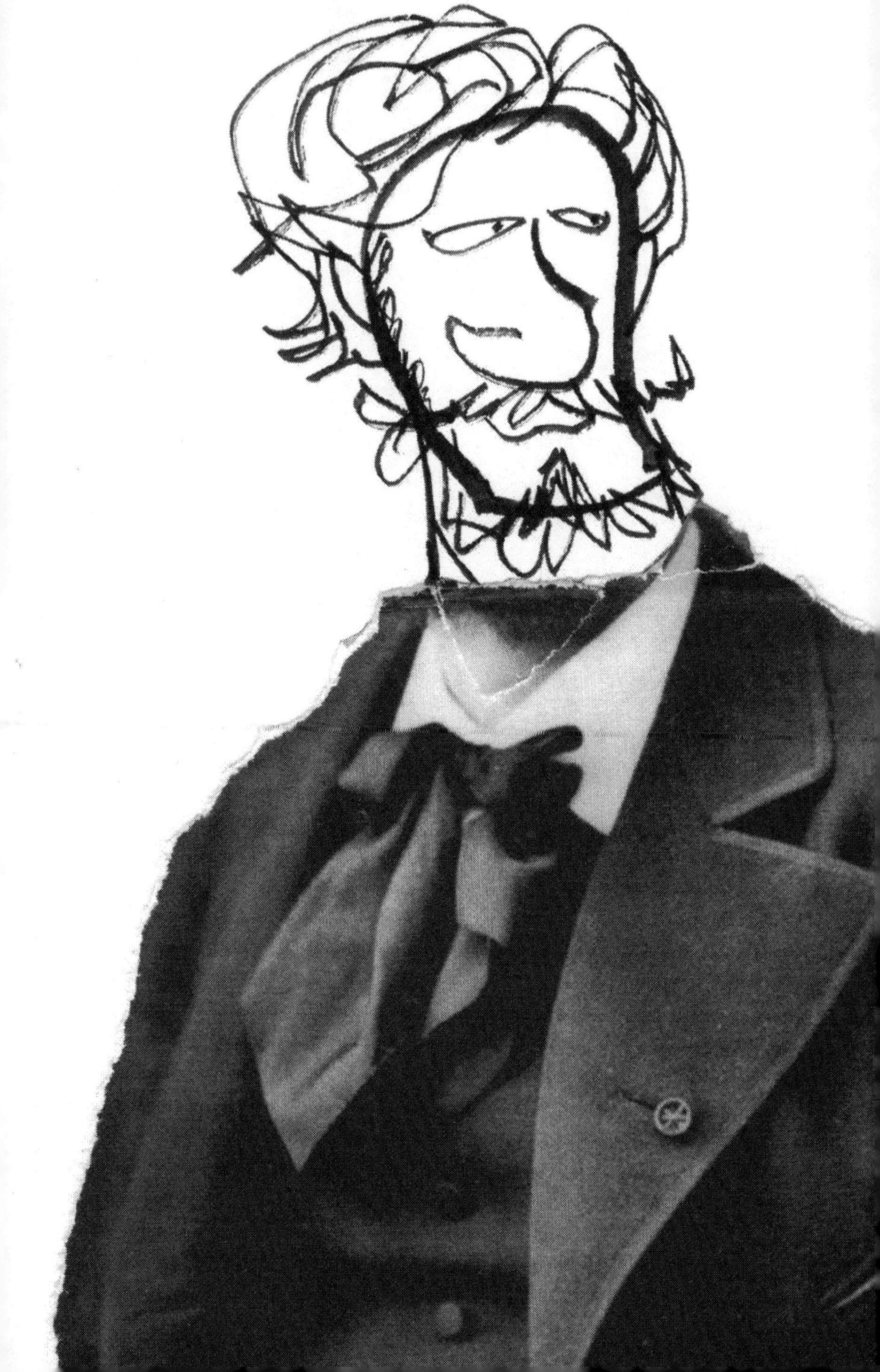

Thank you, Frédéric-Auguste Bartholdi for being inspired to step out boldly and create "Liberty Enlightening the World" as a gift to the United States of America on behalf of the people of France in 1886.

Go 4th!

Personal Declaration of Independence

Today I declare my personal independence from the tyranny of the inner critic, the scaredy-cat who is obsessed about what others may think about me if I follow my intuition: my heart's desires.

I break out of my box with faith: the joyful expectancy that my intuition will guide me in wonderful ways.

From now on I declare my freedom to recognize, trust, and act on my intuitive hunches. I step out boldly.

Signed: _____

Date: _____

Signing this will make me subject to improved health, happiness, love, success, and prosperity, as well as an overall feeling of generosity and love toward my fellows.

A childlike faith gets grown-up results.
So proceed with joy, knowing that
the Universe is conspiring in your favor.

DARRELL FUSARO is an artist, author, and U.S. Coast Guard veteran. He is the recipient of The Army Commendation Medal for meritorious service.

His other self-illustrated books include "What if Godzilla Just Wanted a Hug? Leading with the Heart Instead of the Chin" and "Break Out of Your Box: Be Your Heroic Self."

Currently, he is co-host of the podcast "Funniest Thing! with Darrell and Ed."

foozaro.com

**You've been given the gift of Liberty.
How will you express it?**

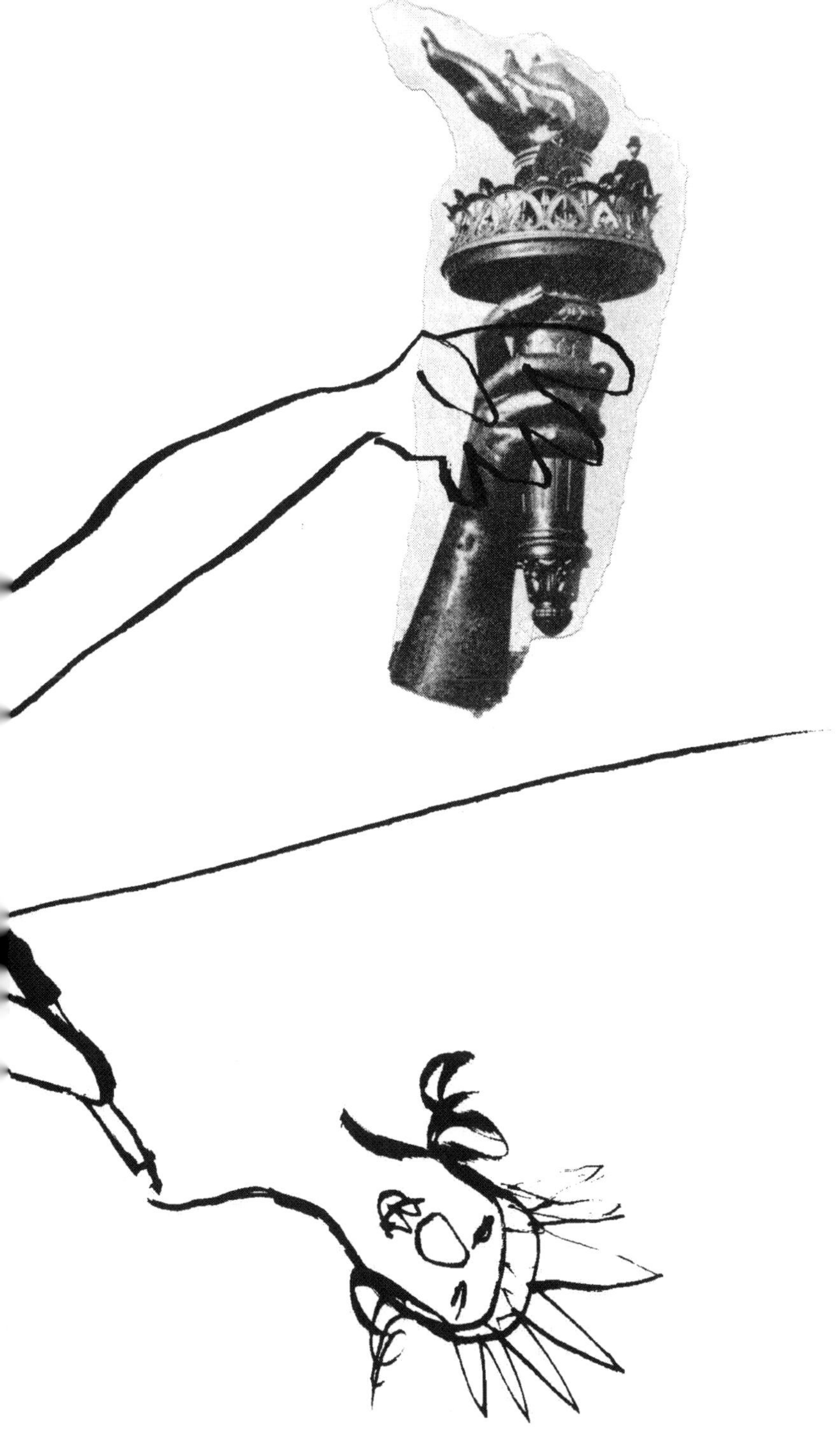

Made in the USA
Middletown, DE
15 November 2024

64342496R10018